Unknown

Anna Rose James
Elizabeth Chadwick Pywell

Stairwell Books //

Published by Stairwell Books
161 Lowther Street
York, YO31 7LZ

www.stairwellbooks.co.uk
@stairwellbooks

ISBN: 978-1-913432-30-0

Cover art: Lisa Findlay Shaw

Table of Contents

Foreword

Thank you for taking the time to read *UNKNOWN*. This collection has come together between two women over a shared love of other women, inspired by those from history and legend who have touched our lives, or the world, and left them changed. We especially wanted to honour those whose names are not often on our tongues.

It is presented in two parts: Myth and History. The poems themselves are, of course, all creative works, where the subjects served as muse, and we wouldn't want the placing of those under History to be read as fact. They are the flights of fancy of two women celebrating, investigating and attempting to reach other women across time and geography.

At the end of the collection you will find an index of subjects, with some detail on the women behind the poems. We hope they will stand on their own as works of poetry, and continue to grow on you with further reading. We hope you will go on to read everything you can about each woman, and perhaps then write your own odes to them.

Anna and Liz

Womanhood

We are ball-busting banshees, battleaxes, old biddies, bimbos, birds, bitches, broads. Cheap cockteases, cocottes, concubines, courtesans, cows, crones, cum buckets, cunts. Dramatic divas, damaged goods, demi-mondaines, doxies, dykes. Emotional Eves, fallen women, fishwives, feminazis, femmes fatales, frigid gold diggers, gossips and gutter sluts. Hags, harlots, harridans, harpies, hetaerae, homely or honey pots. We're hormonal and hysterical. Inamorata. Sometimes we're jail-bait jezebels, or meretrices. Minxes and molls. Nags. Nasty, needy neurotics, nightwalkers and nymphos. Odalisques, ogresses, oiran. Old wives. Paramours and pieces of flesh. Promiscuous prostitutes, if not prudes. Psychos. Pussies. Ribs. We're scarlet women, scolds, sex kittens, she-devils and she-wolves. Shrill shrews, sirens, skanks, skirts, slags, slappers, sluts, snatches and then, eventually, spinsters. Strumpets. Talents and tarts. Tchotchkes that grow to be teases. Termagants. Totty, tramps, twats. Unknown, unknown, unknown. Unladylike, definitely unstable. Viragos, vituperators, vixens. We are wanton wenches, whores and witches. We survive. //

Liz

MYTH

Kore

Sprung forth
from green and blue loins,
as brief as a twinkle
in the eye of a god
of death,
goddess of harvest,
cropped, ploughed, rotivated,
made to yield
libations.

Hellebore
Pig Squeak
False Forget-Me-Nots

Open the jars:
The wine was then drunk.

A new vintage
brings fruits to your tongue.

Bloodroot
Bleeding Heart
Virginia Bluebells

Accounts vary:
a cacophony of whispers.

Enna
Attica
Eleusis

Voices squabble for the discovery of facts.

Ask the man feeding his pigs -
he remembers because they too were
taken by the abyss.

I know the truth to be contradiction;
you cleft the earth,
deeming it irrelevant,
history.

You'll hear my name when you commit to my mysteries -
want it, dread it,
a dawning -
not safe to speak aloud
but galloping:
hecate, Hecate, HECATE!

Did you know that death is also sown?
With care,
grown in the womb of the earth
and foraged, lovingly,
chthonic grasp
on rough bark,
stolen through teenage window,
sliding to muddy roots,
fresh dirt under fingernails.

Lungwort
Creeping Phlox
Solomon's Seal

My mother
will stop the earth from birthing
until I am found.

Perhaps if she had done it sooner,
you would not have made your way up through the ground.

My father,
needing quiet
and respect,
will relent to the noise of the many
and later
restore his place by giving me
grandaughter-daughters.

6

Twinleaf

My lover:
feed me chains of flowers
to hold me in your kingdom,
just some of the time.

I won't ask my daughters with me. ⫽

Gorgo, or Portrait of a woman for whom it will never do justice

Gorgo
Guardian
Protectress
Three sisters
/*Fair-cheeked game*/

He picked the one he knew could be killed.

From the sea I broke forth and in stone I will be-
not buried, but flattened-
after brief,
frantic orchestral
string break.

Shall we talk about how hard he got when he saw me?
You think this is coincidence?
How appropriate that the god of unwelcome wet worms
should set my hair as a cascade of writhing snakes
designed for one purpose: to slay him and his kind.

His kind-
my disgusting kin-

What could he do but destroy me first?
And yet he goes on, detail after spiteful detail:
I have a sword, a bow and arrows, monstrous claws,
a cunt hungry enough to bite off innocent-

/He paints me reaching, seeking, fingers unfurling
outwards-/

–That should have told you something about his story.

He drank his grandeur from my unwilling–
/And just wait til you hear what Freud has to say–/

And just.what.exactly... is wrong with your mother-in-law's
tongue?

Convinced himself he was under a love spell.
/Wicked witchcraft/

Be grateful we're seeking equality, not revenge.
/hatred of mortal man/

If only you could see what manhood it is
that I have faced
/beautifully and terrifyingly/
as they said,
before:
/so terrible that the mere sight could turn a man to stone/

Girls your age
have called it a punishment.

Ironically he made me very hard
to find.
Now...
I drown daily in a timeline filled with his other crimes.
I see exactly how many heads he has crowned with snakes.

I will never return to the water.
I know what it is that brushes my leg.

I will never return to the water.

His friends,
and the woman whose house it was
will send a champion to stop me at the neck.

It is either you or I
who will harden. ⫽

9

Raised by gulls

Their cries drown out the baby's, pull me
to the window where birds are dropping,
crashing into glass with sick thumps
of flesh and beak and claw,
black eyes twisting furiously before they die.

They pile one atop the other,
grotesquely indiscriminate
in their arrangement of bloodied wings,
and I stare, my glassy eyes met by theirs,
outstaring me forever.

When the pact is over and the last
stragglers, finally sensible of the suicidal chaos,
turn and flee, I open the door,
shovel gulls like snow or shit,
watch downy plumes dance like ashes.

Legend says they raised him,
my saintly son, found a doe to suckle,
built him a feather bed. Cenydd,
godly, twisted child of mine,
knows that life was built by me. ⁄⁄

Raisin Sweet-tooth

The breadcrumb trail was inspired, it's true,
but they didn't consider the birds I
summoned and called to my bedside window,
my nod to their desperate hunger. Cries
of salvation and emptiness filled the skies.
Meanwhile I brushed the hearth, unlatched the door
and settled down to wait, the heat up high,
the oven blazing, humming as it roared for
two sour faces, four grubby hands. Appeared,
they lounged as though they owned the place, their cheek
almost as delicious in metaphor
as it would be on a plate. I could feel
the juice in the back of my throat as my
pretty birds nodded, their beaks full of wine. ⁄⁄

Tatterhood

Be with me, dear heart.
Look at the moon, yellow and low
as we ride to church to wed.

Ask me the questions on which your lips stick,

ask me everything except which
witch are you?

I was raised in rags and powdered petals
and I have raised men to bring them to heel.

Do you desire her, my sister, beautiful
in the moonlight? I won back her head
from a pole, stuck it back down with spit and willed

her love to be worth these weeds.
Is yours? ⁄⁄

The Miller's Daughter's Tale

endlessly spinning / spinning endlessly
this could be the spinner's tale / but unlike silver stories
   my gold is
riddled with inconsistencies / cracks threaten sinkholes
while the king threatens me / while the imp threatens me

my mind circles itself / I am sinking in straw
slowly sloughing skin / which I can't afford to lose

spin for me my sinning, singing darling / spin this life away
dress my child in salt and song / if you must must must
I search for your name / slipping through sand and rain

say it sweetheart / sweetheart please ⁄⁄

What you will

Resolved into the figure of a wife,
I understand I am not what I am.
I have doubled; the spaces within me
multiplied into nothingness, and
my heart, become a mirror to preserve
another, who is who she is yet may not be,
cracking under empty pressure,
violet with exertion and pretence.

I stand to both gain and lose
as we two vie for existence.
Neither is real until one lies down to die.
This costume that strangles and protects
could be, I think, cast off and left to decay
in the wreckage on the beach,
and there's freedom in the pain and potential
of naked skin, clean vellum.

When, finally, lightning illuminates all,
I peel it from my body, wet with sea and salt,
leave it piled on upturned rocks
next to the warped wood I sailed in on,
memorialised with weeds and love and history.
Compass broken, I turn and head inland
towards a way to solder the glass,
towards reality, and the heart of Illyria. ⁄⁄

A Winter's Tale

the kitchen fills with you / you fill the bowls
reheated chilli / blankets round our bed
create a mountain pass / uncontrolled
we battle through, dismount / I kiss you, there
and there / we save the stories here, we share
one curling grave and lick the spoons / our feet
are tired and old / I eat your toes, declare
my love / this fortress home is safe, and real

before you smiled, the air was cold / yet now
there's patience in the glass / so very sheer
yet potent, rich and thick / oh! to be known
like this / the mirror cracked and here you are
Hermione / you brought me back to life
and every star here shines for you / loved wife ⁄⁄

The Dancing Queens hear prayers and shuffle their cards

Love me, Queen of the Waterways,
of virtue nonpareil.
Bless me with the gift of your vision.
Rain down your insight
lest I drown in darkness,
alone in blind introspection.

Fly to me, Queen of the Skies,
you who sees all errors.
Judge me kindly with the gift of your clarity.
Blow breezes of truth through me
lest I fall from the mountain top,
alone in condemnation.

Walk with me, Queen of the Clay,
mother of growth and weeds.
Grow me from the seed cell up.
Fill my heart space with hearth,
lest I sleep outwith the walls I called home,
alone in introversion.

Warm me, Queen of the Flames,
as sunflowers dance in your care.
Lead me to lead myself through.
Enchant my lonely dreams,
lest I lose the magic of speech,
alone in cold, dumb silence. ⁄⁄

Ceridwen and Taliesin

Ceridwen
I.

Once upon a time
a goddess - a witch
- a - it was me.

It's hard to say –
my name changed
a few times.

Cyrridfen Ceridfen Ceritven
Kerritven Kyrridven Kerritwen

Ceridwen

my son - Taliesin - was real
- utterly
but I was a myth from conception.

Taliesin
I.

Swallow me up
I'll give you the language of Heaven

      stir your fired mischief brew into
                c o n s t e l l a t i o n s
waves rushing over night sky
      I paddle with clouds and drown among stars

You might call me a Fool but I could teach you a thing or
two,
pull strings that sing like choirs of young lads

Dw i wedi gorffen y gwaith, but there comes no Da iawn
Croeso anyway, Ceri-Bach
Welcome to it all

Ceridwen
II.

You see he was sweet - always sweet -
sweeter by far than Avagddu.

I should have known when I set him to stir
and stir, that he was too

sweet for that little body, that honey would seep
from his bones, that there would be new

life stirring in his veins even before the splash
of inspiration consumed him, and he became you.

Taliesin
II.

I'll come to you as soon as I become
the full face reflected in the broth
Little Gwion has something to prove
I just want you to love me to the bone, Kyrrid-mam
And I know the mist will do it.

Even if I am lost
I will be able to walk on the ripples
Peering down at your daear-body;

Yes, I will bastard you many more times
That is our likeness
A sunken embrace
gulping down towards the dark

Let me see thee in thy woman's weeds

18

Ceridwen
III.

Don't pretend you didn't enjoy my chase,
rage fuelled as it was.

You were more interesting with every curve.
Every transformation yielded more life
- more heat and blood and *poetry*.

He stands before you now the man he is
because I refused to love him until he was ready,
until he was delicious, heavy with power.

And I am here still, he knows I am,
my old bones alone until he visits

when I dress them in flesh.

Taliesin
III.

Hunted,
      Hela,
           Fur,
                Fin,
                     Wing,

finally you catch me up in your gullet
Not the mother's clutch I imagined,
but so much more you:

an enlightenment, the gift of backward birth

I .s.c.r.a.t.c.h. as much from your throat as I can on my way
down

remembering the many   padded feet
that brought us to this place between worlds
within and all around

cwtch me, mami-fen, and see with my eyes
remember what I am made of
when you dress me

Ceridwen
IV.

Ah cariad
I have always seen with your eyes.

In my womb you sang of the skies,
and everything my cauldron fused
became more than magic.

At your birth there was star-song,
the world re-born with you.

Taliesin
IV.

Ceridfen is heavy with the weight of me now
she stoops sometimes, fury swelling with my limbs
/ when I knock /
she says I am singing
though she sends her howls up to the other gods
a reminder:
mae'n dod; hudoliaeth
get it out so I may dash it

Ceridwen
V.

Taliesin makes me monstrous
but his birth changed it all -
roeddwn i ei garu gymaint.

I could not find it in my weak heart
to kill him.

He was of my flesh and of the earth
so by reason of his beauty
I allowed him still to live.

If I had known that he would take his talents
and turn them to immortalising me -

Ceridwen the hag, Ceridwen the witch

I would have dashed his brains on the rocks
in the môr, in the pain of the sea-edge.

But I did not know,
though men lie daily,

and he was beautiful

and I loved him so -
so - unexpectedly.

Taliesin
V.

Bound
wedi rhwymo, I'm within
forever yours
forever bastard

fashioned into hide, and set free to drown
sewn into skin because
beauty makes us terrible

trade our sunken treasures; once, and twice

to be taken up in princely arms
salt water staring into fresh sand
and, at last,
                    b   e   c   o   m   i n g. ⫽

HISTORY

Cartimandua

There are many ways
to back a winning horse

My favourite
    is to chase it from the gate
        roar up its arse and slap the others beside
          with chains and with their perception
        of my kindness

Wifely virtue was never so dirty an asset in another's hand,
    carving not nearly close enough to the ridden ribs as
your own would,
        does, a heaven's reach to a pocket full of
coarse hair

You can top the others as you please,
    grip their bellies with your life-squeezing thighs,
        matting fingers with mane, give 'em a yank
    and a *that's a good boy,*
        fist your loyalties from the baited dusk
        and screw them into these pricked ears

Boudicca can bite my dick

I made my husband a blue maze map of atrocities,
painted to the
        tip of his cock, an army of braying
    bright-billed geese flapping their feet in circles
        while I close them in at the last open
        vein

He was a talker

I made good use of that until his horns came
off in my hands

Can't a man do a god-damn-thing?

25

Slip on my second ring,
       spit my chips onto the plate–
          it's race season again and I'll not break my
       winning streak

             Snap a yew tree as we pass, for my
        pleasure, for his pain

        I'll smile and hand him over

They will never
      see it
        coming ⁄⁄

Of Siwan, who must have been very tired

He had no faith in women so left the dog in charge
while I visited home and he hunted greatness,

forgetting (ignoring) that true greatness
was not in chasing game but in me, Helen, Dafydd.

My instructions were clear: feed Dafydd,
feed Helen, feed Gelert, don't fucking kill them.

It just proves that men, you can't trust them,
which I already knew of course, being a Plantaganet.

I assumed a village Prince, antithesis of Plantaganets
like my bilious father, would be more sensible

but now his beloved dog is dead, insensible
to injustice, and I will forever have to be in charge. ⁄⁄

Fencing

In starched white we still in the morning air,
sweat looping our wrists and temples
like diamonds, I, a Mazarinette, and you,
a princess in waiting.

Circle me, Anne.
I am used to being chased
only do not try to keep me
for I have worn a ring and found it
binding, have fled on horseback,
mannish and weeping
for my children, their mad father.

There are men everywhere
searching out my fortune
and beauty, to hang me on a castle wall.

Kiss my likeness, Anne, the one you carry
around your neck, before you lift your foil
and eyes to me, before we are judged ready,
before en-garde, prêt, allez.
Your feet are light and wet, love,
and I fear you will need them, to run. ⁄⁄

Grizzel

Peeping through the bush atop a bright coral cart,
a topping Tommy hopeful fingers the coin in his pocket,
steeling himself to meet the shaved-faced bear.
Running through a list of cave-born intimacies,
a pick–'n'-mix of parts and paws;
breath baited stales his tar-rag sacs.
Hedge-creeping, he is younger than any man has ever
been.

Inside the market, a far-flung daughter of Nelly
fires a rod between her tongs,
carving it sonsie; an ornate instrument of degradation,
on which she plays most delightfully,
they will say, while they clunk their spilling ale
into each other's cups, across the table
laden with her afore-advertised; over, under, bite.

Mincing is reserved for silvered boys,
not words or pies.
These jollocks pigs are stuck
on her, on how she turns,
glistening under sparks
with an apple in her mouth.
Is she the arsehole, if she chomps?

A stomp of her teeth is a crunch is
absolution of their bon appetite mort–
she'll catch their weeping loss amongst her lashes,
all-overish they'll spit their ichor on her cloth,
draw the long bow across her ham-strings, make them
sing,
meet her earth bath at their bone box.

The youngest of men is ready to feast up from her toes,
hunting for a tail that cannot wag but for him,
for hogmagundy, if it comes.

The guests lay down their knives and forks,
their sit-upons, to lay,
lay down, and sup
of a cwtch with the tallow-ketch.

Nuzzling, guzzling, muzzle her.

A Summer of Celebrations
is about to begin. ⁄⁄

Policarpa

I'll stitch you up good

mea culpa

my mother's eyes were fertile ground
in which to shine

I weave these threads
into my house of abundance

I am childing revolution

that you know as a date in your diary

flowering sabotage
loamy in the gloaming
clever in the dark
let me vegetate your secrets
propagate your propaganda

until enigma blooms forth
showering pollen, spilling its own life on its stem
let me lay it for you
the bias runs this way up

I am the she-wolf you let into your closet
treason is this season

a summer on the eighteenth sea
you may not see me for a thousand years

in the end they took my head from me
to pull the fish hooks from their soup

show me your heritage; I'll show you nothing

people call me out in the rain to attend to the aching pearls
in their mouths
I leave the pain but sneak out with the dirt
leaving them gleaming
a beacon of betrayal

Wrapping my light in royal blue
its richness adorned with golden brocade
folding, beholden to no one
a few darts at the chest
tasteful
    I morph into Gregoria ⁒

Jack

Before man/woman legal boundary
double-speak, she sat above shabby grass,
tucked skirts into drawers, drew imaginary sword,
surveyed man's world and judged it
lacking. Before man/woman legal
boundary double-speak said no, she watched
boys/girls courting, rutting, disgust
in her tears and bones. Before man/woman
legal boundary double-speak cried sin, she
fell in love and love and love with girls
who looked like her in line and curve
and mind, judged them fair. Before man/
woman legal boundary double-speak
thrust and stabbed through realms
of fabric, she watched the life she knew;
knew in young, sad bones she'd have to tear
the boundary designed to keep her out,
rebuild the world. ⁄⁄

Ching Shih

Let me lift your shirt
and kiss the skin beneath it,
fill my mouth with you.
Who can offer you more
than I? Even the sea herself
needs a firm mistress.

Don't leave. Until this storm
has passed, let us indulge in each other.
Indulge me, please.

Now your father is gone
they will look to me and the space
at my side and forget, they will forget,
the number of men whose heads
I have personally separated
from their wasteful bodies.

They will say, who will lead us now?
And I will kill them all.

So help me, my son.
Stand in the vacuum he left
and smile, and I will make you
a king. Or, better, when they write my name
in the history books, so will they write yours.

Let this kiss be my promise. Come,
lift your shirt. Let me
taste the sea on your chest.
Give me your name. ⁄⁄

Buffalo Calf Road Woman

Rosebud battle nurse
I am a sepia rectangle
two black everlasting plaits and a resting frown
wile and vision at my side

If you wait quietly for one hundred years
then creep down the stairs
you will find my act
a gift with your name on it

"The Girl Who Saved Her Brother"
shining and ready to be spoken
your ancestors standing in front of the fireplace
wind-raised wisps of hair on brown faces

The window is closed
where the wind comes
sweepin' down the plain
our stratagem is peace

I got good with a gun
just to show you
how much more I can do
with nothing in my hands ⁄⁄

Ida

Killing in the name of what, I demand to know?

Show me your receipts.
Show me the fingers and nails
of those you have saved.
Are they more precious than my brother's?

The child you left behind with your yellow death.

While you follow ghosts of your white kings
to find enlightenment,
I am here writing letters, one by one,
fighting that we may last to be mist.

Let me tell you what Southern Horrors really look like:
how they drip from the trees.

I took a walk in the woods too,
and visited salvation
in my grandmother's eaves.
The woman whose body
from which you borrowed a cup of sugar.

Snap as many pens as you like; I still have a mouth.

I don't need a desk to prop my words upon,
nor proximity to reach my blood.
It runs where it may but it
will still hear me in its redness. ⁄⁄

Bessie

I think I could be brave for you, Bessie,
if you suffered a flight of fancy
to take me on a tour of my stomach
in the company of clouds,
traversing with the sun and its classmates.

Perhaps we can break a few rules, and bones,
frivolous damage in the wake of our love –
after all, we'll get up again –
this is not your fixed point in time.

Perhaps we can save one of your cracked ribs
and fashion a new disaster of gentler sorts;
a queen of blue and silver in your image.

We have all the sky to roam
but I wouldn't be anywhere except
strapped to your back in this bold tin can
let me be your wingwoman in this
one-room school of hopes and dreams.

Glance back at me with your girlish grin,
a peek of your wanton waggery,
the action of a roguish spirit,
Aéronautique naughty.

Let us paint a jest of physics
in the language of the skies.

Be seen from many angles, like the moon
cameoing in countless windows;
bring the grounded some sharp delicate relief.
Your whole being

a collapse of tension
a trip
an embrace

d i s a r m i n g

freedom.

I find it odd that no one
else remembers your smile;
that the portrait they all
honour is a sombre affair,

separating   from
            you   your body.

I'll always hold the version of you
that I caught in the slipstream,
        the rush of your knowing look,
            a joke shared with a carefree
                look over your shoulder

as if to say,
        Are you sitting comfortably?   *L e t ' s   g   o.* ⁄⁄

Mileva

Second in command,
a great woman behind
a man who was standing in the way.

Owing to time, breasts, accident,
a fraction of a formula
with a perfect score;

an eye for the invisible –
just like him.

Not for figures –
that was his business.

You can say now that I must have been extraordinary
to put these behind me.

Here is an admission of women:
the truth is, I was

but I accepted an admission
of men into my motherhood,
to the power of three.

We even counted on a boy before that,
but we miscalculated,
crunched the numbers,
cut our losses.

Divided,
I wither
with our
daughter

and

without. ⁄⁄

Nachthexen

For Major Marina Raskova

You may call us witches –
it's understandable.

> We're up here on our winged broomsticks,
> tufts of hair from mangy sheep
> given menace by magic,
> given magic by menace.

> We carry silver in our armpits
> and the devil in our ribs –
> we have come to wreak havoc.

> It's colder than our tits out here,
> but why not drink champagne?

You can only die once,
and you can't avoid me –
can't avoid   that witch
                is meant to happen.

I see your eyes are afraid, but my hands are still doing it
anyway –
if you're scared of witches you shouldn't be out in the dark,
kinder.

Come, get your nose scratched at the market.
        We bring our own rulebook to the monastery.
        We don't care about your burning cloaks
                except to keep them alight.

Shooting fish out of a pond.
The devil lives in the still waters, but
                        we are made for the skies.

Call your doctors to inform them of your funerals.

It may be crowded but everyone is happy –
now, do you see how it is better,
to have a hundred friends than a
hundred rubles?

We will make you our tobacco,
pack you down to peat,
smash your foreheads on your god.
We like your enthusiasm.

Dance on the coals and don't blame
your testicles for how ridiculous you look –
it is us little girls who have done that to you –
we just took
advantage of the silence,
followed your gaggle string down
through the rooftops

i   d   l   i   n   g

.   .   .   .   .   .
.   .   .   .   .

The devil made work, and we were looking for jobs. ∥

Althea

Before Serena
and Venus
will follow in my steps,
I plant a kiss on my other self –
beaming from a shiny cup.
I had to be it to see it,
born to Silver but I got my gold –
Rosewater was ready for me.

Take a share in my image, my success –
I am of a family of mixed doubles, after all.
And I know when a victory is my own.
I have nothing to fear from those who try it on –
it does not fit them quite as well.
I am used to playing within boxes, you see;
I learned it from my father, and the police.
It takes a neighbourhood, sometimes.

I set the stage:
all props present and correct –
leaving just enough out of place –
by a degree –
so that a terrible accident might take place –
another Black female on the court –
skimming - the - net –
it might be difficult,
but I made it possible.

Whites washing on boil,
the machine's churning is my backdrop.

What a racket. ⁄⁄

Parul

I am supposed to be writing a poem
    about Mileva Marić –

- but with you quietly homed
in the top-right corner of my screen,

> brown skin glowing
> in the incidental
> triangles of morning light
> your face of concerned
> concentration directed at
> me, long hair free,
> asymmetrical slack-neck
> black top - professional,
> but tired, human, intimate,
> face responding to your work,
> staring up for inspiration...

how am I supposed to write anything but you? ⁄⁄

Jennie

Awaiting a heave   heave of brass –
       -ho–

                 chest –
             its
         puffing
a tuba letting off steam,

         we save our little eggs in a
         dignified skirt-basket,
         called out at age, ready for the ball:
         our mourning autumn wardrobe.

London Season:
     black, brown, yellow and red.

         Our elite retreat high
       above mud-tops
       calls for raindrops to pelt us in
       just the right place,
         scooping us out,
       spreading us wide,
       wine spilled from the goblet –
         little rocks shaken forth
       to multiply fruiting bodies:

           Charlotte   Chloris

           Amelia   Elise

           Magnolia   Evadne

           Anastasia   Orinda

           Felicity   Ninon

Aurilia	Jane
Kitty	Mary
Veronica	Margaret
Artemisia	Betty
Berenice	Dorothy

Disputed by a
shiny-taught-faced
Frenchman, dispersed by rain,

we will take your decaying wood and
turn it into finished young women.

A family of five sisters:
Mya,
didn't come out
yesterday;
Cynthia, Pru;
beg for the
right to curtsy;
the twins, Nid and Nid,
came out last
season.

*We trade in daughters
not shelved yet;
organic matter, fair game.*

*You could try to eat us
but we wouldn't advise it –
we will conquer, or die.

                   Ann Eve
               Grace   Ruth
             Frances   Amelia
              Susan   Sarah
           Catherine   Eleanor
           Emeline   Rebecca
            Isabel   Bridget
            Rachel   Judith
            Phoebe   Fanny
            Agnes   Ellen
            Martha   Nancy
             Peggy   Sally
              Lydia   Rose
                 Ada Mary

We imagine,
        in the moss,
                what shapes we could
                    form with the boys. ⁄⁄

Khadija sees

The sun streams and
                warps
blinds
blink
      ing
refracting through glass
in - unrestrained - wayward joy
over photographs
                paper walls
sepia caught by the edges,
lettering in gold and love,
sight saved by framing

her eyes, seeing, open to the end
of time even in the dark
room where we

                blink
closed ours. ⁄⁄

Index of subjects

MYTH

Kore (Persephone) - Queen of the Underworld, Goddess of Spring and Rebirth (The Eleusinian Mysteries, Greek Mythology) - 41st-18th century BCE - *Anna*

Gorgo - Medusa, Gorgon sister of Ovid's *Metamorphoses* and other iterations (Greek mythology) - 8th century BCE - *Anna*

Raised by gulls - Saint Cenydd of the Gulls and his mother - 6th century - *Liz*

Raisin Sweet-tooth - witch from Hansel and Gretel - collected 18th/19th century - *Liz*

Tatterhood - Norwegian fairy tale - collected in 19th century - *Liz*

The Miller's Daughter's Tale - Rumpelstiltskin's victim - collected 18th/19th century - *Liz*

What you will - Viola, *Twelfth Night* - 16th/17th century - *Liz*

A Winter's Tale - Hermione, *The Winter's Tale* - 16th/17th century - *Liz*

The Dancing Queens hear prayers and shuffle their cards - based on the Tarot - 19th century - *Liz*

Ceridwen and Taliesin - Welsh poet and his mythological mother - 6th century - *Liz and Anna, respectively*

HISTORY

Cartimandua - first-century queen of the Brigantes - 1st century - *Anna*

Of Siwan, who must have been very tired - wife of Llewellyn, who killed his dog Gelert - 12th century - *Liz*

Fencing - Hortense Mancini, lover of both Charles II and his daughter, Anne - 17th century - *Liz*

Grizzel - Grizell Steevens, philanthropist, benefactor of Dr Steevens' Hospital in Dublin, and rumoured Pig-Faced Woman - 17th/18th century - *Anna*

Policarpa - Policarpa Salavarietta - 18th/19th century - *Anna*

Jack - Gentleman Jack, a.k.a. Anne Lister - 18th/19th century - *Liz*
Ching Shih - famous Chinese pirate who married her own son - 18th/19th century - *Liz*
Buffalo Calf Road Woman - Brave Woman, a Northern Cheyenne woman who saved her wounded warrior brother, Chief Comes in Sight, and her husband, Black Coyote - 19th century - *Anna*
Ida - Ida B. Wells, African American journalist, abolitionist and feminist - 19th/20th century - *Anna*
Bessie - Bessie Coleman, early American civil aviator - 19th/20th century - *Anna*
Mileva - Mileva Marić, Serbian physicist and mathematician and the first wife of Albert Einstein - 19th/20th century - *Anna*
Nachthexen - Major Marina Raskova and the all-female military aviators of the 588th Night Bomber Regiment, Serbian Air Force, WWII - 20th century - *Anna*
Althea - Althea Gibson, American tennis and golf pro - 20th century - *Anna*
Parul - Parul Bavishi, Editor and co-founder of the London Writers' Salon - 21st century - *Anna*
Jennie - Jennie Hallam-Peel, Chairman of The London Season (debutante balls) - 21st century - *Anna*
Khadija sees - Khadija Saye, photographer who tragically died in the Grenfell fire - 21st century – *Liz*

Acknowledgements

Grateful acknowledgements are made to the following publications, in which some of these poems first appeared: *The Selkie* (Womanhood), *Kalopsia* (Raised by gulls), *Dare to Create* (Tatterhood), *Analogies & Allegories* (Raisin Sweet-tooth), *Visual Verse* (Khadija sees), *Bi Women Quarterly* (Parul).

Anna would like to thank Harriet Cash, Marc Brüseke, Lizzie Huxley-Jones, London Writers' Salon, Shell Cousins, Eliza Hunton, Jimmy Parker, Addie Johnson, Edith Kirkwood and Alice Serne.

Liz would like to thank Poetry LGBT, London Writers' Salon, ARVON, and Anna, the most inspiring co-writer possible. Also my children, Eloise and Henry, who are always showing me new ways to see the world, and Jade Mutyora, for whom I write every poem.

We would both like to thank our Out on the Page poetry peers, particularly Christian, Caroline and Chris, who provided so much valuable feedback and encouragement for these poems.

About the authors

Anna (she/her) is a queer, bisexual actor-writer of mixed British and Asian heritage, based in North Yorkshire. As well as poetry, she writes flash fiction, memoir and scripts for stage and screen. Her previous works include *Little Irritants* (Analog Submission Press); *Love, Alberta*; *Wayside*; *100 Friggin' Poems*; *It's Ok to Fall For Camp Boys* (self-published). Her work has also been featured in at *The Best New British And Irish Poets Anthology* 2019-2021 (The Black Spring Press Group), *Writing East Midlands Writers' Conference 2021, 330 Words, Alpha Female Society, Blue Animal Literature, Calm Down Magazine, Dissonance, Enclave, Forever Endeavour, Gingerbread House, Global Poemic, Mookychick, Prismatica, Vagabond City Lit, Visual Verse* and *What Rough Beast*. You may know her face from Sonnet Sisters and Six Lips Theatre, or her voice from *Tin Can*.

Elizabeth (she/her) is a York-based poet and writer of short stories and flash fiction, and an English and Drama teacher when she's not writing. She also runs creative writing groups for children. She has recently been published in *14 Poems, Impossible Archetype, Fat Cat Magazine, Writing East Midlands Writers' Conference 2021, The Selkie, Tipping the Scales Literary Journal, Drawn to the Light Press, Lazy Women, Forever Endeavour, Dare to Create, Analogies & Allegories, Outta Time Magazine, Kalopsia, Visual Verse, Nightingale & Sparrow, Mookychick, Ang(st)* and *Dreich*. She had two poems nominated for the Pushcart Prize in 2020, and she sometimes performs at open mic nights in York when the country's not in lockdown.

Other anthologies and collections available from Stairwell Books

For further information please contact rose@stairwellbooks.com
www.stairwellbooks.co.uk
@stairwellbooks